formatio

TRADITION. EXPERIENCE.
TRANSFORMATION.

Formatio books from InterVarsity Press follow the rich tradition of the church in the journey of spiritual formation. These books are not merely about being informed, but about being transformed by Christ and conformed to his image. Formatio stands in InterVarsity Press's evangelical publishing tradition by integrating God's Word with spiritual practice and by prompting readers to move from inward change to outward witness. InterVarsity Press uses the chambered nautilus for Formatio, a symbol of spiritual formation because of its continual spiral journey outward as it moves from its center. We believe that each of us is made with a deep desire to be in God's presence. Formatio books help us to fulfill our deepest desires and to become our true selves in light of God's grace.

 **Spiritual Formation for Individuals and Groups**

SPIRITUAL FRIENDSHIP

MINDY CALIGUIRE

An imprint of InterVarsity Press
Downers Grove, Illinois

InterVarsity Press
P.O. Box 1400, Downers Grove, IL 60515-1426
World Wide Web: www.ivpress.com
E-mail: email@ivpress.com

InterVarsity Press® is the book-publishing division of InterVarsity Christian Fellowship/USA®, a student movement active on campus at hundreds of universities, colleges and schools of nursing in the United States of America, and a member movement of the International Fellowship of Evangelical Students. For information about local and regional activities, write Public Relations Dept., InterVarsity Christian Fellowship/USA, 6400 Schroeder Rd., P.O. Box 7895, Madison, WI 53707-7895, or visit the IVCF website at <www.intervarsity.org>.

All Scripture quotations, unless otherwise indicated, are taken from the Holy Bible, Today's New International Version™ Copyright © 2001 by International Bible Society. All rights reserved.

Design: Cindy Kiple
Images: Radius Images/Jupiterimages.com

ISBN 978-0-8308-3510-2

Printed in the United States of America ∞

P   20   19   18   17   16   15   14   13   12   11   10   9   8   7   6   5   4   3   2   1

Y   23   22   21   20   19   18   17   16   15   14   13   12   11   10   09   08   07

CONTENTS

INTRODUCTION

At one time, my soul suffered from a severe case of malnourishment. During a time of painful circumstances, when important relationships became confusing, I experienced disillusionment with my high ideals and a clear lack of control. I felt numb, as though my body just kept going through the motions of my life, but nobody was "home" inside. It was hard to connect with God, and in truth I had stopped even wanting to try.

A part of what my soul needed to avoid this deep slump was right in front of me, but I resisted mightily. While I felt strongly that I didn't need *more* people in my life, I desperately needed at least one soul friend. I needed a friend who knew my history, who knew my weaknesses, who celebrated my strengths and who knew God intimately. I needed an intimate, life-giving relationship that would help me pay attention to the activity of God in my life and help me respond.

Many who eventually became such friends in my life were right nearby, but I had never allowed myself to open up to them, nor had I learned how to be that kind of friend to someone else. I knew how to be a leader, helper, encourager, coach and follower, but those roles are not all that we're made to be. I did not know how to be a friend.

By God's design, far beyond our "roles," we are highly relational beings. Even those of us possessing the crustiest exterior have an intrinsic need for human connection. It's simply the way we are made—in the image of God. And while that explains many of the amazing qualities of the human soul (like the sophistication of our imagination, reason and communication), our being drafted in the likeness of the triune God also implies a unique and necessary way of relating. We are made for meaningful relationships in which we open ourselves wide to one another in self-giving, nonhierarchical, mutual love.

So why do we—why did *I*—resist intimacy with others if it's part of the soul's architecture? Usually, we don't have to look too far for the answer. Think for a moment: what have caused the greatest sources of pain in your life? If you're like most people, the deepest wounds and the greatest traumas did not result from random financial reversals or even from a tragic accident or illness. The vast majority of our deepest hurts stem from relationships.

Whether we were abandoned, betrayed, ignored, rejected, abused or marginalized, the deepest scars on the human soul are those received at the hands of other people. People we knew. People we trusted. People we "let in." Years, decades and, in some cases, entire lifetimes later, the pain associated with those relational scars can feel as fresh as the original wound itself. The human soul does not recover easily from a blow to our point of connection; sometimes it does not recover at all. Perhaps, even as you read these words, certain names and incidents spring to mind—you have known this to be true in your own life as well.

But did you ever wonder why people—relationships—have the power to wound us so deeply? to scar a human being for life? Put very simply, it could never hurt that deeply or shape us that greatly or remain with us for that long unless that place inside us is the core of who we are—the core of the way we are. When we become wounded at our point of connection with others, we become wounded at the very core of our identity.

If you are old enough to read these words, you are invariably among those of us who bear the invisible marks of soul wounds dealt by the hands of others. And you are old enough to have caused a few of those wounds yourself. No two ways around it, relationships are painful and messy.

When we recognize the need to care for our souls, then the very last thing we'd want to do would be to put ourselves back into that precarious place of reaching out to others. I know it wasn't exactly at the top of my list. Why on earth would we venture such a risk? The safest place to be, it would seem, is alone.

Or is it?

I hope to change your mind.

Using This Book

This book is divided into four experiences: "A Source of Spiritual Power," "Barriers to Soul Friendship," "Forging a Soul Friendship" and "Going Deeper." Within each experience are four distinct parts that can be used as daily readings (though some parts are longer than others). The parts build on each other, so you'll want to read one part at a time and take time to reflect on the questions embedded within the text.

Giving yourself a day or two for each of the parts should allow you to comfortably complete one experience in a week and the entire guide within about a month. Each of the four experiences is followed by a discussion starter if you wish to share this with a friend or small group.

The other Soul Care Resources book available—*Discovering Soul Care*—will allow you to explore specific ways to care for your soul with greater intentionality.

"A truly loyal friend sees nothing
in his friend but his heart."

AELRED OF RIEVAULX

EXPERIENCE ONE / *A Source of Spiritual Power*

1 PATH FOR GROWTH

Many of us realize the importance of prayer for building a deeper relationship with God. The study of Scripture, too, is a classic and necessary element of spiritual growth. Times of solitude, along with a host of other valuable spiritual practices, can also be helpful.

All of these have in common the ability to help your soul get quiet and be open to the power and love only available in God. In those times, the human soul "cracks" open, and the Spirit of God moves to shape and heal, woo and nurture, correct and direct the inner being—far below the level of words. God's Spirit is doing "soul surgery" on a willing patient. Amazing!

Soul restoration—soul transformation—happens. But it requires both our own and God's involvement. Like a joint project we work on together, there are things God "brings to the table" and there are things we bring. God brings the love, the power, the vision for who we are and who we are becoming (basically God brings most everything), but we must bring our part as well: openness.

■ When was the last time you sat down with God? What do you recall being significant about that time?

■ What kinds of things usually help you be willing to connect with God authentically? For some it might be time in nature, for others worship music and for others silence.

Spiritual practices help us actually sit down with God. They help us get quiet internally, and they help us lean in to better listen and receive from God. When the love and power and radical goodness of God are welcomed deeply into the human soul, things start to happen! We actually become more loving, less self-centered; more sensitive, less calloused; more generous, less greedy. Over time we become effective in whatever role God has for us in extending his love, grace and provision to the hurting world around us.

There are times, however, when the limits of individual spiritual practices become exposed: times of great tragedy, of spiritual or emotional fatigue, or of just remaining stuck spiritually. I've experienced them all. What do you do when you can't stand the thought of praying, when the words of the Bible seem plastic and false? What about when you've been doing everything "right" and the bottom falls out? When the ministry initiative fails? When a child dies in a freak accident? When a spouse says, "I'm leaving"? When the ropes of addiction still bind you even when you know all the right theology?

These are the times when spiritual friendship can still connect us to God.

Now, while I am not saying that authentic relationships magically make various troubles disappear, I *am* saying that when we are isolated in the midst of these circumstances, we are closing ourselves off to one of the primary mechanisms by which God will touch our lives.

Human relationships are bumpy. We fail one another regularly. But the fact remains that God has mysteriously endowed each of his followers with the presence of his Spirit so that when we live openly and honestly with at least a few others, we also necessarily open ourselves directly to the power and love of God.

What if we could learn to open ourselves to God in completely new ways? What if he longed to meet with us in the eyes and ears and arms and voices of his flawed and imperfect people who are just like us? What if we could look into the eyes of a friend and see just a glimmer of the love of God? What if we didn't need to work so very hard to say all the "right" things to friends who seek advice or wisdom? What if?

Of course, the experience of spiritual friendship need not be a last resort. I hope that one day God's people will naturally view open, healthy relationships as one of the most vital dimensions of spiritual life and health. That will require a revolution of sorts—a long-overdue revolution. I'd like to invite you to your own personal revolution. Learn new ways of relating. Don't worry about changing your entire family or church, just begin with yourself. Are you willing to take that challenge and begin a revolution of one (that would be you)?

■ As you consider forging or deepening some friendships in the future, what resistance or hesitation do you sense (if any)? What hopes are raised? Take a few minutes to talk with God about that in the space below, being sure to invite his guidance and direction as you pursue this study.

■ Imagine yourself sitting down at a table with God to talk about soul friendships with him. What would you like to say? What, if anything, do you sense God would like to say to you?

Ordinary friendships are generally characterized by intimacy, trust and mutual enjoyment of one another. Spiritual friends share those qualities, of course, but are also characterized by another element: spiritual friends actively help us pay attention to God. Similar to the way other spiritual practices connect us to God, our soul friends help us sit with him. They have the capacity to help restore life to the soul.

■ How is this kind of friendship similar to or different from what you have experienced with friendships in the past?

What is it about these friendships that makes them so powerful? Beyond the human element, something of a spiritual nature is going on in this kind of friendship. It's invisible but it's absolutely real.

Ephesians 4:16 says, "From him the whole body, joined and held together by every supporting ligament, grows and builds itself up in love, as each part does its work." The writer of this passage uses the metaphor of a human body, whose parts are intimately connected to one anther (joined by ligaments—connected), to describe how spiritual growth occurs among Jesus' followers.

■ How do the interconnections in our physical bodies facilitate growth (for example, the connection between the wrist and the arm, or the skin and the blood)?

■ What exactly causes the growth once these connections are in place? That is, what is the source of power?

Our connections with God and each other make the whole process of growth possible. Only the power of God can change a human soul. When members of the body are meaningfully connected to each other, they feel each other's pain, and they sense each other's joy. And when they are open to it, in a mystical way that is deeply embedded in ordinary human conversation and circumstances, the Spirit of God has unchecked exposure to the soul of each.

The Spirit of God moves freely between those in the body of Christ who are thus connected, and without any direct effort to cause these changes, growth, transformation and healing naturally occur. The direct effort comes in forging that kind of relationship in the first place. Then, because of our intimacy with God and each other, our ordinary, flawed selves can be part of a transformative work that happens deep within our hearts and souls—and those of others.

Larry Crabb writes in his book *Connecting:*

Releasing the power of God through our lives into the hearts and souls of others requires that we both understand *and* enter into *a kind of relating that only the gospel makes possible. . . . This kind of relating depends entirely on deep fellowship with Christ and then spills over on to other people with the power to change their lives, not always on our timetable or in the ways we expect but as the sovereign Spirit moves.**

■ How do you respond to this quote?

■ What about the gospel makes this kind of relationship possible?

---

*Larry Crabb, *Connecting* (Nashville: W Publishing Group, 1997), p. 5 (emphasis mine).

19

We can expect to experience God's power at work in soul friendship because of God's indwelling presence in the lives of his people. How does this work?

When a person enters into a relationship with God through Jesus, Scripture teaches that a radical spiritual phenomenon takes place in the life of the new believer. The interior world of a Christ-follower is invaded—a willing invasion, but an invasion nonetheless. The new Christian has become an "outpost" of God's presence here on earth as the Holy Spirit takes up residence in the human soul.

■ Consider the words and actions of Jesus in the Gospels, the ways that he interacted with people and the message Jesus brought. What was Jesus known for? What characterized his life?

■ Who stands out in your mind as someone who has embodied at least some of these characteristics of Jesus—a friend, mentor, parent or even a figure from history?

■ What words or phrases describe what *you* are known for?

A curious word describes the presence of God among his people: his *kingdom* dwells among us (Luke 17:21). What might that mean? Well, by the presence of his Spirit, his kingdom now dwells individually inside his people, but his presence is also active between us. There is a supernatural dynamic to the relationships between all people—especially between those who share a faith in Christ. Among followers of Christ, the Holy Spirit is flowing, energizing, healing, convicting and transforming.

What does that mean for our daily lives of faith and relationships? First, it invites us to engage in deeply spiritual living as individuals, to fan into flame the personal relationship we enjoy with the God of the universe. When we have that intimacy established with God, it changes who we are and how we operate in every way. Thus, it cannot *not* pour out of us into others. John 15:5 (NASB) explains this dynamic well: we "abide" with God. We have an intimate, dependent relationship with God as our source of life, and we cannot thwart or stop what it is God intends to do through us. We are completely available to allow his Spirit to flow through us into the lives of others.

Second, the spiritual realities of indwelling call us toward each other with greater expectancy and willingness to experience God working among us—working precisely because we've ventured into the kinds of relationships through which his Spirit can powerfully move.

- How would you describe your current level of expectation that God's Spirit would interact with you through a friend and vice versa?

- Write about a few experiences that might have influenced that level of expectation.

Not only are these relationships possible, but within them lies the hope for an outpouring of the Spirit of God in our day—transforming the souls of individuals and accomplishing the purposes of God in our own lives and in our world.

- If this is relatively new for you, or even if you already enjoy this kind of relationship, how do you imagine your life might be different through deeper connections to a few soul friends? What would be the same?

Soul friendships, while receiving their extraordinary power from God, possess some clear and consistent human characteristics. What marks the kind of relationship through which God can freely move among us? Many factors contribute, such as honesty, self-awareness, genuine love and acceptance, but soul friends are also characterized by being open (or undefended), authentic and "unagendaed." Under these circumstances, your soul is literally opened up to another person in a mutual way, and this is what makes transformation by God's Spirit possible.

Open or undefended relationships transcend the invisible system of calluses and emotional armor that generally keeps the self protected from other people. That invisible system of protection is our defenses, which are elaborate and strong, and very important in many settings. But in an open relationship, the defenses gradually come down, and we allow our true self to be known.

"Unagendaed" relationships occur when we drop our agendas for what we want from other people and just connect with them as they are. Often we have unspoken agendas for other people. We may not even be aware of them until we find ourselves angry or disappointed in someone—and realize they just weren't meeting our expectations. When I am tempted to move toward friendship with someone I enjoy but from whom I also want something, that's when an agenda creeps in.

Relationships marked by these qualities throw open wide the gates for the Spirit who indwells each one of us to move freely. Most of us learn this slowly, but we can make progress toward this kind of relationship. When we love other people for their own sakes, we become concerned for their well-being, for their future, for their freedom and for their lives. We want them to "win"; we want them to experience everything God has for them. We are absolutely *for* them—for their growth, for their happiness, for their freedom, for their being exactly who God has made them to be. Nothing more and nothing less.

However, even when that desire is awakened in us, on our own we remain completely powerless to ever really break the barriers our friends may have in their lives. But because of our relationship with them, because of mutual openness and trust, the soul has "cracked" just a bit more and God moves deep within—at a level far below words. Supernatural power is released.

■ Did you ever have the distinct impression that God was speaking to your heart through another one of his followers? Describe the circumstances surrounding that experience. Who was it, what did you sense God saying to you, and how did you respond?

■ Have you ever had a sense that God was working directly through you in someone else's life? What happened?

The potential power of the Holy Spirit being poured into another person's heart and soul depends on your own deep fellowship with Christ. What words would you use to describe your current experience of intimacy with Christ?

When we remain deeply connected with God, one of the realities of the spiritual life is this: We cannot *not* bring his person and presence into every circumstance we find ourselves in. He's there because we're there. That's the miracle of indwelling. Furthermore, we don't have to work so hard at being like Jesus, and we don't have to think so very much about what Jesus would do; because of our intimacy and yieldedness, over time we simply act and behave as he would because that's what makes sense to us. Things that characterize the person of Jesus will eventually begin to characterize us. Our minds are being renewed; this is the miracle of transformation taking place. And when we bring that very-much-in-process-but-open-to-God self into relationship with others, all heaven breaks loose!

But it all hinges on our own intimacy and surrender to God.

■ In what ways do you suspect that your own character is being shaped in a way that is more like Jesus? Have you found yourself more compassionate lately? less anxious?

■ What tends to keep you close to the heart of God during ordinary days? Are there certain practices or places that remind you of God's presence and love? What are they?

■ Talk with God right now about your desire to remain connected. Prayerfully ask, *What is one simple thing I could do today to pursue a deeper connection?* (Be sure to listen!)

God can touch our souls when we are relating with one another. I am with God when I am with my soul friends in open and unagendaed ways. If we could let down our guard and learn to relate this way, what might happen?

5 GROUP DISCUSSION

Summary

God created humans in his own image, which includes his very *essence* as community. We are designed to enjoy and to develop mutual relationships of self-giving love, just like the Trinity. But the pain and brokenness and disappointments of life often leave us deeply isolated, unwilling to extend ourselves relationally. Yet intimate relationships remain one of the primary ways God intends to be present with us and among us. We tend to forget this! And our souls suffer for it, our communities suffer for it, our world suffers for it. Developing a few soul friends—intimate, life-giving relationships that help us pay attention to God—can help us experience the new life available in God. The incredible power of soul friends to bring healing and transformation into our lives hinges in the reality of God's indwelling Spirit in the lives of his people. When, as individuals, we remain deeply connected to God and then develop relationships marked by openness, authenticity and the lack of a hidden agenda, the power of God freely moves in and among us.

Discussion Basics

This discussion guide works best in a context of openness and vulnerability among friends (new or old!). Before answering the opening question, if you don't know each other already, take plenty of time to exchange names and some basic get-to-know-you information—like where you live, what kind of work you do, what your family is like and maybe something silly, like your favorite childhood cartoon or book. At the end of the study, you may also want to exchange basic contact information, such as telephone numbers and e-mail addresses. However, before you begin, a few ground rules are in order.*

First, please feel no pressure to answer any of these questions. I encourage you to be vulnerable, but if at any time, for any reason, you don't feel comfortable, it's okay to pass.

Second, please give one another the gift of listening, not advice. This is not the time to tell about when that same thing happened to you or about the Scripture verse that "solves" that problem. Ask a follow-up question, perhaps, or simply remain quiet—but refrain from interjecting your own advice.

Third, no faking. There is no need to be anything other than who you are. If what's really true feels too uncomfortable to talk about, just take a pass. Trust in the process of authentic, vulnerable communication with God and others.

And last, ruthlessly protect and honor one another's confidentiality. When a friend shares an intimate struggle or concern, it represents a gift of their trust. You can even thank them! But it was given to you, not to everyone you know, so guard your words accordingly.

Opening

What brought you to the place of wanting to do this study at this time in your life?

---

*Adapted from John Ortberg and Ruth Haley Barton, *An Ordinary Day with Jesus Leader's Guide* (Grand Rapids: Zondervan, 2001), pp. 32-33.

Discussion

1. What, if anything, did you sense God stirring in you through this first experience?

2. Go back over your written responses to parts one through four. What one or two ideas stand out as something you'd like to bring to the group? Why did they stand out to you?

3. Place yourself on a spectrum of how you view relationships: "intimacy is dangerous" versus "intimacy is desirable." Describe something in your life that may have influenced that belief.

4. Read John 16:7 and John 17:26. How do you experience this indwelling reality in ordinary life? Are you largely unaware? often aware?

5. Which of the three characteristics—openness, authenticity or lack of a hidden agenda—comes most naturally for you, and which is most difficult?

6. Talk about one thing that you anticipate might be a challenge for you personally in the coming days or weeks.

Prayer

If you feel comfortable, have one or several group members close this time in prayer, perhaps using this text from Ephesians 1:17-19 as your guide (interestingly, the language throughout this prayer is plural—"you" is directed to a group of people, not a person):

I keep asking that the God of our Lord Jesus Christ, the glorious Father, may give you the Spirit of wisdom and revelation, so that you may know him better. I pray also that the eyes of your heart may be enlightened in order that you may know the hope to which he has called you, the riches of his glorious inheritance in the saints, and his incomparably great power for us who believe.

Before the next gathering, everyone should complete "Experience Two: Barriers to Soul Friendship."

"By this everyone will know that you are my disciples, if you love one another."

JOHN 13:35

EXPERIENCE TWO / *Barriers to Soul Friendship*

1 FINDING ONE CORNER

God is raising an army of people—his followers—to offer irrefutable evidence for his very existence. He appears to have bet the farm on this one—likely because he knew that relationships characterized by love, grace, compassion, generosity and forgiveness could only be explained by a power greater than human nature: his own. In truth, we have historical evidence that such radical communities have periodically existed and become irresistible attractions to those who were seeking an authentic source of life. Of the community that developed immediately following the earthly presence of Jesus, it was said they "enjoy[ed] the favor of all the people" (Acts 2:47). New believers flocked to this first fledgling community that was marked by love.

Unfortunately, it seems very few pockets of these counterculturally harmonious and loving groups exist today. And where those communities do exist, they are so rare and episodic in nature that most intelligent observers rightly consider them an unusual reflection of a few remarkably good-hearted people—not the occurrence of anything as pervasive and universal as the very nature of God. After all, if God is the same everywhere, always, we would expect these attributes to be seen more frequently and consistently among his people.

False. Plastic. Insular. Judgmental. Image-oriented. Hypocritical. Full of disdain and irrational fear. Basically, as Christians we have become known as the very antithesis of the grace that ought to characterize Jesus' people. We fight among ourselves, becoming increasingly irrelevant to the world around us—irrelevant to the very ones we're supposed to win over.

The love of Christians for one another was supposed to have left an indelible impression on the lives of those far from God—those whom God was drawing toward himself. And, indeed, we have left an indelible impression but not the one we'd hoped for. It would appear that most spiritual seekers want little, if anything, to do with the Christian faith on the basis of what they can observe from the way we treat each other.

Are there any widespread communities characterized by truth and grace in this world? Interestingly, there is one kind of transformational community whose participants fairly consistently experience a significant measure of personal growth across generations, cultures and individual histories. These kinds of communities embrace dependence on God's grace, and they hold out hope for the real possibility of healing and a life of renewed peace and purpose. Sadly, but not surprisingly, these groups fall under the disdain of many in the church. I am talking about twelve-step communities.

People in twelve-step communities come to accept that they are powerless. They come to see that they are dependent on God or a higher power. They know that they need grace. As a result, these people are transformed to the extent that they embrace this path of life. Typically gritty and gut-wrenchingly honest, the quest for "real" and "authentic" is clear. "You are only as sick as your secrets," you'll hear. That sounds a lot like Jesus! Similarly, one of the anchor values of recovery is a certain kind community, the essence of which is relationships marked by grace and truth that underpin and sustain those finding freedom from addictions.

Is it any wonder, then, that many of those in twelve-step recovery groups have a realistic pattern of authentic, spiritually based transformation and the millions of seemingly "together" but isolated and defended Christians sitting in pews every Sunday morning do not? The army of the church, the body of Christ, should look a great deal more like the recovery program it is intended to be and a great deal less like the country club. In my travels I've discovered that this is not exclusively a North American phenomenon. Around the world, many of Jesus' people are wrapped tightly in a strait-jacket of external conformity and hiding. All too often we are stuck in a prison of our own making, pitifully useless to the desperate needs of the world around us and absorbed in our own smug illusions of self-righteousness.

Is it no wonder that those far from God take no heed, sensing no divine pulse among us? Why would they?

Isn't it time this changed?

I am not suggesting a subtle "tweaking" of our direction here. What is needed is a radical shift at the very core of how we view and approach relationships. Perhaps this idea is as appealing to you as sudden immersion in an ice-cold ocean. Though it may feel like it will kill you, take heart—it may be the very part of you that needs to die so that you can finally begin to live. Then the truth and self-giving love of a living God will be seen in and through you.

So hang on! I'm telling you, that water could feel cold and uncomfortable at first, but you still need to jump.

■ What's one of the riskiest things you've ever done? What happened as a result?

■ Have you ever encountered a community of Jesus' followers who were marked by grace and truth? What was or is that experience like for you?

■ Take some time (perhaps writing in this space below) to talk with God directly about this kind of community. If appropriate, acknowledge the times when you personally have been more inclined toward judgment or pretense than toward authenticity and grace.

Henri Nouwen, a Catholic priest and writer, masterfully articulated the difficulties we find in forming authentic community. In his book *Intimacy* Nouwen wrote,

> *We have probably wondered in our many lonesome moments if there is one corner in this competitive, demanding world where it is safe to be relaxed, to expose ourselves to someone else, and to give unconditionally. It might be very small and hidden. But if this corner exists, it calls for a search through the complexities of our human relationships in order to find it.**

Two key ideas emerge for us from his insightful words: the need for safety and the need for a search. We long to find a safe place to be ourselves, to let down our guard, to be accepted and loved for who we really are. But we will most likely have to search intensely in order to find it.

■ What keeps us from feeling safe with each other? (What keeps us from being open and undefended with others?)

■ Does the idea of a search for this "corner" ring true with your experience? Why or why not?

---

*Henri J. M. Nouwen, *Intimacy* (San Francisco: HarperSanFrancisco, 1981), p. 23.

A friendship can become a safe place where you are fully known and unconditionally loved. It can be a place where your story, including your brokenness, flaws and failures, is known and accepted. On the other hand, a friendship can also be a place where your story is known and condemned. Or known and spread. Or known and rejected. Or known and ignored.

The pain of those betrayals of trust can convince us to become and remain isolated for decades. We put up impenetrable walls of defense, thinking they will keep us safe from relational wounds. Unfortunately, those walls also open us up to a host of other evils, such as self-absorption, distorted perceptions of truth or inertness regarding the purposes of God in the world. Simply, we are made to thrive in relationship.

As we seek to develop soul friends, it can help to develop our awareness of what makes relationships "safe" in the way that Nouwen described. Typically, the things that make us "unsafe" with one another are listening poorly, giving advice, trying to fix, lacking empathy and self-disclosure, rejecting, manipulating, betraying, judging, gossiping. What's behind these things? Fear of really knowing ourselves, pride, lack of self-awareness, competition, envy, jealousy, resentment, self-hatred, insecurity or a sense of superiority—a whole host of attitudes.

Ever been on the receiving end of one of those? Not surprisingly, these toxins not only kill the relationship into which they are released but also often sabotage our efforts to build relationships elsewhere. Once betrayed, it is very difficult to trust again. Once abandoned in a time of weakness, we struggle to ever let someone see our shortcomings again.

So if we will venture into the uncharted waters of soul friendships, we'll need to search for safe people with whom it's reasonable to take the plunge. What will we be looking for in a safe person? Henry Cloud and John Townsend offer three hallmark qualities of a safe person in their book *Safe People:*

1. They draw you close to God. Safe people do not try to take the place of God in your life by providing "answers" or solutions. They do not try to be your everything. Safe people understand your dependence upon God and gently draw you in the direction of receiving what you can and must from God directly. They encourage your spiritual development; they're quick to remind you that God cares, that God is at work, to encourage your full surrender and participation in whatever it is God might ask of you.

2. Safe people also draw you close to others. This is significant in that a safe friend will not try to isolate you from your other important relationships. Safe people are for your marriage, for your work relationships, for your friendships beyond themselves. When appropriate, they gently push you towards resolving conflict—not merely allowing you to vent your frustration.

3. And last, safe people draw you close to your true self. This is perhaps one of the most difficult to observe, and most powerful when working right. Many of us live lives of relatively deep deception

about who we actually are, both the dark and the light. A true, safe friend can see where you are stuck and also see your potential— and they join the fight for your soul's freedom from the barriers so that you more closely resemble the person God envisioned when he made you.*

Soul friends do not try to become God and direct the processes of our growth and development. Instead, through an authentic, unde-fended, unagendaed way of being together, God's Spirit works among us, between us and through us in such a way that the barri-ers are broken and freedom is found.

■ Do you have awareness of safe people in your relational network now? Who might they be?

■ How would you rate yourself on each of the three qualities of safe people?

■ In what ways have you offered those qualities to others?

Safe People (Grand Rapids: Zondervan, 1995), p. 143.

■ Describe a time when you didn't respond to a friend in a way that was safe. What happened to the relationship?

Consider reading Henry Cloud and John Townsend's book *Safe People* to go deeper into these questions.

3 KNOWING WHAT TO LOOK FOR

Many times people are surprised at the thought that friendship "qualifies" as a practice that has the power to help us grow spiritually. Why is it a spiritual practice? Why is it something that we would intentionally pursue? Because this kind of friendship—soul friendship—will not just "happen" of its own accord. Effort will be expended on our part—we will need to work toward this kind of relationship. There's joy to be had in friendship, for sure, but there's effort too!

A spiritual practice can be thought of as *anything* I intentionally do to become and remain open to the ongoing work of God in my life. Often it involves carving out precious time and space from cluttered schedules. Forming a spiritual friendship will certainly need that kind of focused attention and intentionality.

For many people, it begins with an intense search, as Nouwen puts it, "through the complexities of our human relationships."* What are we looking for? Here are three factors to keep in mind.

Energy. Do you come away from time with certain friends feeling more energized than you do after you've spent time with others? Who are the people in your life that give you energy?

■ List a few names here.

---

*Henri J. M. Nouwen, *Intimacy* (San Francisco: HarperSanFrancisco, 1981), p. 23.

You could say these friends are "life giving" to you. They may be people quite a bit like you in season of life or personal background, or they could just as easily be people who are very, very different from you in terms of personality or lifestyle. But what you're paying attention to is not how much you have in common but rather the effect on your energy level from the time you've spent together.

And beyond your energy level, some people may just naturally leave you with a greater sense of spiritual vitality. One of my friends describes these friends and these experiences as ones that make her want to "run hard after God." I love that imagery. She is one of those people for me; when I spend time with her, I come away more eager to discern God's activity in my own life and respond fully. Nothing about our actual conversation is directed toward her trying to convince me of this response; it's just simply the way I feel after we've shared time, stories, screw-ups, concerns and dreams.

Matching. After you identify someone who has that intangible energizing factor in your life, you'll want to begin the process of exploring the possibility of deepening the relationship. One indicator I've learned to pay attention to is this idea of "matching" intimacy levels. This concept was formally introduced to me by a mentor several years ago, but I had intuitively recognized this dynamic in relationships. I expect you will as well.

One woman told me about her experience in a friendship of continually opening up deeper and deeper areas of her soul until she finally realized what was wrong in the relationship: her friend never reciprocated. The friend listened attentively but did not match the vulnerability level. As a result, the relationship became stagnant. When you risk vulnerability with someone else and reveal yourself a bit more intimately, it can be helpful to observe whether your friend matches your dive or not. A relationship that is growing in openness and intimacy will continue to take new risks, and those risks will be mutual—not one-sided.

There are many reasons for withholding intimacy, but regardless of what they might be, withholding intimacy is a sign that a relationship is not moving toward becoming a soul friendship at this point in time—and the sooner you realize and adjust your expectations, the better. Do it without anger, without judgment, but with an honest recognition of what *is* and a willingness to let go. This does not necessarily mean ending *any* relationship with this person but it does mean letting go of the expectation of a soul friendship with them.

Be sure to entrust yourself to others who are willing to journey with you in vulnerability and intimacy.

Confidentiality. Every friendship is vulnerable to breaches of confidentiality. And when confidence is broken, whether a betraying friend tells the truth or not, the damage is often irreparable. For those in more public leadership roles, the risk of betrayal threatens to shatter entire careers or ministries.

Is it any wonder this fear is what keeps so many people silent about their private struggles? To be sure, the danger is real. For this reason, one of the things you must consider in a prospective friend is their capacity to hold confidences.

Some people have found it helpful to give their prospective intimate friends a "confidentiality test." I know this happens, because early on in my adult years I was given just such a test! Thankfully, I passed it, but I remember feeling just a bit odd when I realized what had happened.

The test involved my friend sharing something more personal in nature with me—but nothing personal enough that would have put her at risk had I failed the test! A few weeks later she checked in with me and point-blank asked if I had shared this bit of information with anyone. My answer was "No, you asked me not to!"

Her next words have remained with me ever since. "Mindy, I want you to know what I was doing. I just gave you a confidentiality test, and you passed!" She continued, "You need to realize that many people may want to be your 'friend' for a variety of reasons, not all of which may be good. In addition to that, there are well-meaning people who simply cannot keep a secret—they are not bad people or evil people, they just can't keep a secret. But you need to know that ahead of time, before you've entrusted something to them unwisely. You, too, will need to learn how to give people a confidentiality test."

It's okay to give a prospective friend a low-risk confidentiality test. Believe the best in others, but be wise. Some people cannot keep a secret. Of course, you also should want to do whatever it takes to become the kind of person who can keep confidences for others.

■ Have you ever been wounded by a breach of confidence? If so, how did that impact the relationship?

■ What role does fear of exposure play in your life now?

When the elements of safety are in place, friendships freely flourish—even under the most unlikely circumstances.

One of the best examples in the biblical narrative of a functioning friendship actually took place between two people who definitely had ample reason to hide behind the barriers we have identified. They were men whose place in society should have caused them to be direct competitors for position and power, and they were extremely public people—at even greater risk for the damage of betrayal.

A famous prince and a famous warrior. They would have been relentlessly followed by all the paparazzi of their day. They were about as popular and as public as you could be in 1500 B.C., and they should have been adversaries. One stood to inherit the kingdom, but the other had been destined by God to take over and rule. The king himself, in jealous rage, had attempted to assassinate the warrior on several occasions. (For the full story, read 1 Samuel 18—20.)

In spite of all this, though, God knit their hearts together. They are described as intimate, soul-level friends. They were "for" each other when they really could have been against each other.

What can we learn from them? Somehow, King Saul's son Jonathan and Saul's most successful warrior, David, overcame these potential barriers in favor of vulnerability and relationship. We'll learn more about their friendship later, but for now recognize that no matter how unlikely your circumstances, those circumstances do not categorically prevent you from experiencing a soul-level friendship. It just may save your life.

■ Have you ever observed an unlikely friendship, similar to that of David and Jonathan? Who was it between? What made it work?

■ When you scan through the complexities of your human relationships, are there certain people you automatically cross off your mental list of prospective friends simply because of their position, role, "different-ness," proximity or anything else?

■ If you had been David, what would have been the hardest thing for you to overcome in getting to know and trust Jonathan? What if you had been Jonathan?

5 GROUP DISCUSSION

Summary

As exciting as the prospect of intimate, life-giving friendship may be, the hard reality is that we also fear it. And for good reason. Sadly, Christian communities are not characteristically known for being places of acceptance and authenticity (though I hope this will change). It is vitally important, then, to honestly consider the barriers to soul friendship. One barrier is the lack of safety in a relationship. What kind of person is it really wise to open up to? Someone who draws us closer to God, closer to others and closer to our true selves. Another real barrier can be the time, effort and risks required to really search out and then build this kind of relationship. But when the right ingredients are in place, an intimate and life-giving relationship—one that helps us encounter and respond to God—can emerge and truly grow. In the Bible, David and Jonathan—two men who should have been adversaries—stand out as a shining but rare example of intimate soul friends.

Opening

How have you been doing since we last gathered as a group? What have you noticed about relationships?

Discussion

1. What, if anything, did you sense God stirring in you through this second experience?

2. Go back over your written responses to parts one through four. What one or two ideas stand out as something you'd like to bring to the group? Why did they stand out to you?

3. Return to "Part Two: Finding Safe People." Discuss your responses to the questions in this section.

4. Describe someone who typifies a safe person. What makes you willing to open up to this person?

5. What unsafe characteristics are you most susceptible to?

6. What is the biggest barrier for you in forging this kind of soul friend-ship? Does the story of David and Jonathan offer you hope that your barriers can be overcome? Why or why not?

Prayer

If you feel comfortable, have one or several group members close this time in prayer.

Before the next gathering, everyone should complete "Experience Three: Forging a Soul Friendship."

"But only those do we call friends to whom we can
fearlessly entrust our hearts and all our secrets;
those, too, who, in turn, are bound to us
by the same law of faith and security."

AELRED OF RIEVAULX

EXPERIENCE THREE / *Forging a Soul Friendship*

1 MIRRORING

Years ago, I worked as a sales representative for a Fortune 100 company. We lived at that time in Simsbury, Connecticut, and on one crisp January morning, I had a sales appointment with a prospective client in Massachusetts—a two-hour drive. I decided to finish getting ready in the car, so I threw my cosmetics bag into my car along with my briefcase. The bright sunshine danced across the mounds of New England snow on either side of the highway, and my love for nature and winter took over. I listened to my favorite music and sang along with complete abandon, totally forgetting that I hadn't put on one smidge of makeup.

After an hour or so in the car, I remember noticing that my lips were chapped from the dry winter air and the car's heater. So I looked in the console of the car and discovered a tube of lipstick that someone had given me. I would never have purchased this particular kind of lipstick on my own both because of the cost (a very expensive brand) and because of the color (bright orange). But I kept it since it had been a gift, and also because, due to the quality, it felt great on very dry lips.

So as I was singing my heart out, I put it on like Chapstick. All over my lips and around my whole mouth. Felt great.

Eventually, I arrived at the client's site and conducted my sales call as scheduled. On the way out of their building, I stopped in the ladies' room before heading back to the car. And there to meet my eyes in the mirror was one of the most ridiculous-looking people I have ever laid eyes on. Not one speck of makeup but for the bright orange lips, which looked like Bozo the Clown, and wearing a bright red jacket. Why didn't anybody tell me? I felt like a fool, but I was quickly able to laugh at the ridiculousness.

But what about the times when it's rage, discontentment, superiority or insecurity that's all over my face and everyone but me can see it? Then it's no longer funny; it's tragic. These things can be perfectly obvious to anyone around us, but at times we are unable to see them. We can't see ourselves at the precise time when we most desperately need to see the truth about ourselves.

People can mirror to us those things about ourselves that we simply cannot see, for whatever reason. Sometimes mirroring reflects truths that are difficult to hear: "Mindy, why do you always seem rushed?" Sometimes it is deeply encouraging. In either case, when these truths are offered in the context of unwavering love, they are life giving.

Soul friends can be safe mirrors who help you see the truth about yourself and love you enough to walk with you to a place of healing and life. They are *for* you. *For* your life. *For* your freedom. *For* your growth and maturity.

They don't want you to miss one thing that God has for you, so they're willing to tell you the truth about yourself—if you're willing to hear it. And they can be a vital channel through which the very person of God may work in the depths of your soul.

Mirroring conversations between loving friends provide the authentic, fertile soil for spiritual growth to take place. These kinds of conversations have the effect on our souls of helping us sit down at the table of transformation. They help us stay in that chair just a bit longer, and they help us come to God more open and yielded and willing.

There are times when we invite mirroring from safe people whose perspective we trust. During times of transition, or during times when we feel particularly "stuck," the observations of a loving friend can often help us see what we can't. Sometimes—though not always—these friends do have an insight or perspective that can immensely help us grow. All it takes is the willingness to ask.

Sometimes a friend will even lovingly take the risk to venture an unsolicited observation in the hope that it will stimulate growth and life. Friends have loved me enough to say, "Mindy, I noticed that you and Jeff (my husband) were especially frosty with one another the other night at small group. It looked as though you were in a lot of pain. Do you want to talk about what's going on?"

Many times friends are the ones who call out in us gifts and dreams we barely know are there. They help us see how God may be working through us in a particular situation; they provide an inviting atmosphere in which we can really dream out loud about our future.

Sometimes, though, they call out the darker themes. They see the fear in our eyes. They hear the resentment in our choice of words. They feel the weight of our hopelessness. By helping us see those, they also help us turn toward God.

Here's an opportunity to practice a bit with the idea of mirroring:

■ Think of a close friend of yours or someone close who could develop into a soul friend. What's something you observe about them that you're pretty sure they don't know to be true about themselves? Remember, this could be a way God uses them in positive ways or an attitude you suspect they're unaware of. Write about it below, as though you were speaking directly to them.

■ Now think about an area in your life that you're pretty sure you're not seeing clearly. It could be confusion you feel about a relationship or an ongoing conflict or temptation that continues to hold you hostage. What would you ask that friend for? What do you wish you could see more clearly? If it's hard to imagine such a vulnerable conversation with a real person, then imagine asking God. What would you ask God to help you see if he were sitting in that chair next to you?

■ As you imagine having these two conversations, how do you find yourself reacting?

■ How do you think these kinds of conversations might open the door for God to work more deeply in your soul?

2 SELF-DISCLOSURE

Most relationships don't start at the advanced level of mirroring. While that's the picture of intimacy, trust, vulnerability and spiritual authenticity we're aiming at, it's generally not where we start. The intense curiosity we express toward one another begins in the less dangerous waters of simple "getting to know you" kinds of conversations. These conversations matter; they're not just killing time to earn the right to the deeper stuff. When we explore other human beings, we are developing a deeper understanding of how they're wired and what they think. Each clue along the way helps us to understand the other person and, ultimately, love them more. At their most basic level, soul friendships are born out of self-disclosure. That disclosure deepens over time to include the areas that are spiritually sensitive, but we don't have to start there.

One of the easiest starting points with another person is to just get to know their personality. What makes them tick? This is a rich area of interpersonal understanding and can help foster intimacy. Whatever grid you use, it will be fruitful.* Of course, nothing fancy is really needed. Just an inquisitive spirit and a listening ear will do!

I find that some people are naturally quite self-aware; others loathe

---

*Several I'm aware of are the Myers-Briggs Type Indicator, Enneagram, the Gallup Strengthsfinder, the DiSC and the love languages books by Gary Chapman.

that kind of introspection! We all can make a concerted effort, though, to gain a more objective perspective on what we're like. It is often helpful to use a series of questions to help the process, so reflect on your own personality, on what makes you tick, by answering the following questions (if you don't like being asked in the first place, that will tell you something about yourself too!):

■ What do you know about your own personality? For example:

> Are you introverted or extroverted?
> If you like to read, do you prefer fantasy literature or tend toward biographies or historical fiction?
> What do you enjoy for fun?
> What tends to be a pet peeve for you?

These kinds of questions, and a hundred others, can be very valuable to explore on your own and are then terrifically fun to share in a growing friendship.

■ What questions do you typically ask when you're getting to know someone better?

■ How well do the answers help you discover that person's personality?

■ What else might you ask to learn more?

A second, somewhat more personal, level of self-disclosure comes when we get to know about a friend's family of origin. Some grew up in military families; others lost a parent to death or divorce. Some folks grew up in the same house from the day they came home from the hospital as a newborn; other families frequently moved homes and states and even countries. You can learn a great deal about others by asking questions like, Did you grow up in a family with wealth or a family that struggled financially? Did your family have a strong faith or none at all?

As you learn about a friend's family of origin, you can begin to understand just a bit more of what the world looks like from their perspective—to look out at their world and try to see what they see. Understanding people's family of origin helps you identify with them, care about them and love them. When you reveal those things about yourself, it helps your friends identify with, care about and love you too.

Below are a few questions to consider as you think of your own family of origin.

■ What adjectives best describe your growing-up years? See if you can write at least fifteen.

■ What were your parents like?

■ What was your birth order among siblings (if any)?

■ What was the spiritual tenor of the home?

■ What were your friendships outside the family like?

■ What was your view of God as a child?

■ What aspects of your family of origin are most difficult for you to let others see? How might (or how does) being known in those areas influence your life? your spiritual growth?

The following questions will guide you in processing what you know about a friend's family of origin.

■ Think of one close or growing friendship in your life. What are a few facts about that friend's family of origin that have helped you understand them?

■ How has understanding your friend's history deepened your friendship?

3 AREAS OF STRUGGLE

When the hope of a friendship extends beyond the fun and enjoyment of companionship into the realm of the soul, the process of self-disclosure often leads naturally to the places of greatest challenge: our areas of struggle. Some would say that women more naturally dwell in this relational territory, but I find that any relationship that truly begins to delve into our spiritual life needs to go there.

Whether we struggle with materialism, negativity, resentment, self-acceptance, prejudice or irresponsibility, our friends provide a safe place in which to talk about our challenges as well as the efforts we are making to turn these areas over to God's care. Often, as we learn more about our friends' personality styles and family of origin, their areas of struggle begin to make more sense. "Of course," we might say, "No wonder it is so difficult to trust again, or try again, or rest in God's goodness." That kind of understanding can lead to transformation.

Talking about our areas of struggle, as helpful as that can be, still falls short of one of the most important kinds of interpersonal conversations that directly contributes to transformation: confession. This term may be loaded with all kinds of history or negativity for some of us, but the sooner we can make friends with the concept, the sooner we can get on with the business of living the kind of life Jesus makes possible.

We find the theme of confession throughout Scripture. James says it most clearly: "Confess your sins to each other and pray for each other so that you may be healed" (5:16). Is there really a spiritual link between confession and healing—whether emotional healing, spiritual healing or even physical healing?

■ How do you respond to reading James 5:16? Is the idea of talking and praying in this way appealing? intimidating?

■ Does the hope of healing James offers seem valid for your circumstances? Why or why not?

Interestingly, twelve-step recovery groups anchor much of their transformational path on this concept. Confession is recognized as a necessary step in the path of recovery. That is, you'll never experience wholeness beyond your willingness to face the truth about yourself and expose it. Similarly, a theologian friend of mine once said, "The only real barrier to spiritual growth in our lives is unwillingness to face the truth about ourselves." Bit of a chilling thought, isn't it?

A helpful way for me to think about confession has been to recognize that it consists of three parts: (1) an acknowledgment of the wrong that was done, (2) a "confession" that I was the one who did it and (3) a willingness to go public with this fact. We say, in effect: "Here's the line. Here's where I crossed it. I need to be known in this." As embarrassing and vulnerable as these conversations, I am becoming willing to have them when needed, to ask a friend to hear my confession.

The phrase "I need to be known in this" is a powerful one. If you're like me, this is not exactly what you'd call a "felt need." Nothing in me wants to be known where and when I have failed. Instead, I want to hide. But at a deeper level, I know this: if I want to grow, if I want to heal, if I want to be free, then "I need to be known in this." So I become willing to move toward confession.

Eventually, true soul friendships are characterized by this very gritty and honest freedom to acknowledge areas of brokenness and sin. There is a shared thirst for freedom, understanding of the spiritual power of confession and a "whatever it takes" mentality. And when you and a friend give it "whatever it takes," you can be sure that freedom and transformation are not far behind.

■ Write a few words about an area of your life that has been a perpetual struggle for you. What would freedom really look like in that area? How badly do you want to be free? Are you ready to let go of your image?

■ This will be a difficult question to answer, and it doesn't necessarily apply to everyone, but are there some secrets that have kept you sick for too long? If you feel comfortable doing so, write (in code if you have to) about those secrets here, and then use this space to speak with God directly about the influence of those secrets on your life so far. Again, speak honestly, but be sure to listen for God's response as well.

Closely related to the idea of self-disclosure and confession is our *response* when we hear one of those moments of honesty and revelation by another. When one human being chooses to authentically express the truth about who they are, that is holy ground. In such a moment, the Holy Spirit's activity is present, even if the topic represents an expression of failure or pain or confusion. We need to respect this and respond to it.

Unfortunately, the reaction we often have to another person's struggle or sin reinforces why they might have feared self-disclosure in the first place. I find there are two particularly unhelpful, even destructive, extremes to avoid.

At one end of the reactionary spectrum, when we hear the truth about our friend, the temptation exists to recoil in horror. When people finally come to the point of "coming clean" with a struggle such as pornography, addiction to alcohol, affections for someone other than their spouse, cruel anger toward their children or a dozen other sins that we abhor, we may very well be in shock. We can't believe what we're hearing. As a result, we resist, and it shows. We'd rather not hear it. We don't *want* that to be the truth about our very together-seeming friend. We often go to the place of horror or shock—hating what we see in another—because, at our core, we still resist grace despite our supposed beliefs. We resist our own need for grace, and we thus resist other people's need for grace as well.

Sitting with friends over the past few decades, I've heard in painful detail about the exact nature of mean-spirited, vengeful actions, wandering hearts, angry words and self-destructive choices. Sometimes I still need to swallow hard or curl my toes in my shoes when I hear those things. But my reaction is my own immaturity, and while I can be honest with my friends about how hard it may be to hear those things, I want to be present with them in a way that receives their confession as a fellow struggler—which I very much am—who deeply respects their choice to bring their darkness into the light.

I've learned, from those who've responded to me this way, to always thank them for sharing. We can genuinely do this for each other, even when we have no idea what else to say (which is a good place to be). We can always thank our friends for being willing to entrust to us this essential ingredient in their own development, and we can encourage them, reminding them that exposure is the key first step toward freedom.

On the outside, you and your friend sitting in a coffee shop or walking the fairway, having a conversation may look very ordinary. However, once a struggle has been exposed or a sin confessed, we know that in the unseen world, untold spiritual power has just been released. God is at work. This is holy ground . . . take off your shoes. And watch, prayerfully watch, what unfolds.

■ If you have had this experience, describe a time when confession played a role in one of your friendships. Were you the one confessing?

receiving a confession? How did you feel during the conversation, and what has happened since then?

■ Have you ever found yourself recoiling in horror as someone else shared an area of struggle or sin? How did you respond to that person?

■ If you've had the experience of someone recoiling in horror at something you've confessed, how did that reaction influence your relationship with that person? How did it influence your relationship with God?

It took me a long time to learn how to be comfortable with uncomfortable conversations. In years past, I had no idea how to sit with myself or others in those moments. I used to react to this darker form of self-disclosure the same way I'd react to someone who was bleeding. When they came to my small group and began, in my thinking, bleeding all over the table, I did what seemed right: I put forth every effort to stop the bleeding! I used to think, *Hey, you're getting blood all over the table! It's getting all over me, over the others in this group, and it's getting all over you! And we can't have that . . . it's messy, it makes stains, and it seems dangerous.*

My solution in those days? I used to believe that certain verses in the Bible had magical tourniquet powers—slap the right Bible verse on the bleeding person, and the blood flow will stop. In hindsight, I shudder to think how many people were hurt by such "leadership."

How did I grow? On the few occasions when I had the wisdom to shut up for a few minutes rather than pull out my first-aid-kit Bible, I listened to how a few others responded to those who were bleeding. I observed women who approached blood differently than I did. They weren't alarmed by the mess; they moved toward it. They actually went after the source of the bleeding in a way I had never experienced or seen before—it got even messier! But I noticed something else over time: their efforts helped people get well.

I had been about the business of keeping the room clean; they were about the business of healing. So I became their student for a while. Now, when I see someone bleeding all over the table, I have much greater confidence in the healing work God is doing. And, as you might have guessed, my own deep internal bleeding now has a safe way out.

So while we don't want to recoil in horror at the blood, the other extreme to avoid is this: do not minimize. Don't pretend it's not there. When someone risks their "image" to expose an area of struggle or sin, many nice and well-meaning folks respond by minimizing their venture into confession.

We might say, "Anyone would struggle with that; it's no big deal;

don't worry about it." Even if it seems quite small to you, it is a big deal to the person and to God, and we should respect it as such. And when it actually is a big deal, we still run the risk of minimizing. A conversation like this is very serious, very risky and very important.

When a friend heard me confess about something related to one of my children, she—having no children of her own—had the perfect opportunity to minimize my confession. Many parents do this with one another. Instead, my friend thanked me for sharing this with her, reminded me that my words were a signal of the deeper activity of God in my life, looked deeply into my eyes and said, "Mindy, you're forgiven. That's why Jesus had to die. You're forgiven."

How deeply I needed to hear those words! I needed to receive that forgiveness, to remember the truth, to let my anxious, striving shoulders down and just receive grace. But honestly, I also wanted to kick her under the table! "It wasn't that bad," my pride screamed from somewhere inside me. I was aware of that interior pushback, but I was more aware of how it felt to be reminded that God's Son hung on a cross to take away the sins of the world. He paid the penalty so that I could be released from guilt and shame and restored into relationship with God, to make a way for me to become a different kind of woman. My soul "cracked" just a little, and I felt the movement of grace. I was opening myself up to change, and it happened because I went public with wrongdoing—and received grace. She didn't tell me it was no big deal.

When someone brings a confession to you, be sure to remind them as well, "That's why Jesus had to die. You're forgiven." They may want to kick you under the table at first, but your eyes and voice will deliver a message their soul desperately needs to hear from God.

■ When you hear those words of forgiveness, how do they strike you today? Are you in need of forgiveness right now?

■ Please use this space here to come clean with God if you feel the need right now. He will neither recoil in horror nor minimize your sin. You will be fully known, fully loved and fully forgiven. That's why Jesus had to die. You're forgiven.

5 GROUP DISCUSSION

Summary

Soul friendships emerge out of the fertile soil of knowing and being known. Soul friends can help us know ourselves better by mirroring to us the truth of who we are. So how do you get to know a soul friend? And how well do you get to know a soul friend? Two very important questions. Helpful ways to get to know your friends better include discovering the design of their unique personalities. What are they like? What do they like? How do they make decisions? Those kinds of questions, from a variety of sources, will help you and a friend really get to know each other. So much of who we are today springs up from our "roots," so it can also be helpful to explore your friend's family of origin. But when a friendship is going beyond ordinary levels of intimacy and moving into more spiritual territory, two additional areas become important to share with a soul friend: our areas of struggle and, even more specifically, our areas of wrongdoing. Soul friends share the joys of life as well as the struggles, and their ability to both divulge and respond to a confession opens the doors to radical transformation. There is freedom to be had!

Opening

How have you been doing since we last gathered as a group?

Discussion

1. What, if anything, did you sense God stirring in you through this third experience?

2. Go back over your written responses to parts one through four. What one or two ideas stand out as something you'd like to bring to the group? Why did they stand out to you?

3. Return to "Part Two: Self-Disclosure." Describe your responses to the questions in this section.

4. How does talking with a friend about areas of struggle differ from confessing sin? What kinds of struggles are you more willing to disclose? What areas of struggle (be as specific as you feel comfortable!) are more difficult for you to raise?

5. Read James 5:16 aloud. What, if anything, has been your experience

with confession—especially confession to another person, not only to God?

6. During your time together or before the next gathering, have each person develop an individual "spiritual timeline" that creatively depicts the various events or seasons of their life, noting what their experience of God was during those times. Take time in the group for each person to talk through his or her timeline. This could take an hour or more for each person, so plan accordingly! Alternatively, you could pair up for these conversations prior to the next gathering or save it for a mini-retreat. This is a terrific way to get to know a soul friend's history.

Prayer

If you feel comfortable, have one or several group members close this time in prayer.

Before the next gathering, everyone should complete "Experience Four: Going Deeper."

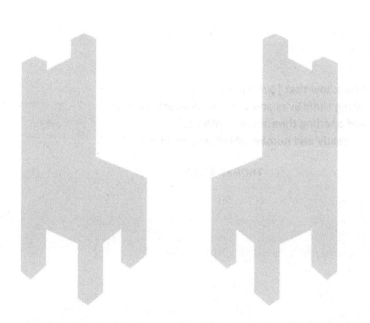

"We know that [our friends] are with us,
lifting their lives and ours continuously to God
and opening themselves, with us,
in steady and humble obedience to Him."

THOMAS KELLY

EXPERIENCE FOUR / *GOING DEEPER*

1 PRAYING FOR A SPIRITUAL FRIEND

At this point, you may either be feeling grateful for the intimate friend-ships you've sustained over the years and eager to go deeper, or you may be feeling depressed to discover that this kind of relationship is available but somehow has eluded you thus far.

If you lean toward the latter description, know that your desire for deeper and more authentic connection with others is good. In fact, it's normal. It is the kind of living God wants for you. While moving to-ward relationships in new ways will likely raise fears and involve new behaviors, the path is a good one and one in which you can count on God's help.

That's a good place to start, actually: with an honest assessment of what "is" in your life right now and an honest request to God for a soul friendship to start or deepen.

Take a few minutes to thoughtfully and prayerfully reflect on your past and current relationships.

■ Describe an intimate life-giving friend you currently have.

■ What do you appreciate most about that person?

■ Describe a painful ending to a relationship. What happened, and why?

■ What makes you feel understood or heard by a friend?

■ What do you especially desire right now as it relates to friendships?

One of the first natural places to turn in building a soul friend is prayer. How so? It may be that, for some, the prospect of finding another person with whom to share their truest selves raises a boatload of pain. They tried once or twice before and failed, or they were abandoned and rejected, or they simply see no one in their relational world who seems to share a desire for authenticity and spiritual growth. Loneliness itself is their constant, gnawing companion—if they still retain the capacity to feel.

For others, the walls of defense have been in place for so long that the nerve endings, which would have signaled isolation and loneliness, have all but deadened. There is no pain; they are numb. My own journey began with numbness, not a desire for intimacy. *What on earth would I want that for?* I wondered. But I was so broken I couldn't pretend any longer, and my friends received me just as I was. Either way—whether you're eager to build new friendships or still a bit hesitant—you were not meant to live in isolation, and I hope you are ready to take a next step.

I do not know how God might provide the person who could join your journey, but I do know a God who routinely moves such mountains and who is particularly interested in meeting you right at this tender place of openness to relational connection. So an entirely appropriate place to begin is prayer.

■ In the space provided below, speak with God openly about what you want, what you resist, what your fears are and what you wish to experience in a friendship.

Scripture urges us to bring our requests to God frequently, even relentlessly. If this is a current area of growth for you, consider incorporating a reminder to pray for friendships into your daily routine. Is there a logical time or place for you to anchor your prayer resolve? It may be that you will assign the noon hour as a time when you could briefly direct your attention heavenward, asking once again for God to provide. Or perhaps place something that symbolizes connection to you on your desk—maybe a spare computer cord! Then, when you notice it, it will remind you of that desire and motivate you to prayer once again.

Remember, as you're praying for an important area of your life, pay close attention to the things that begin to happen around you. Keep your heart especially open as you ask God to provide soul companions. They may not look like the kinds of people you thought God would provide, they may not live in the places you expected or do the things you imagined, but stay open.

If you are fortunate enough to already have a deepening friendship, prayer is also a very natural way to build and intensify the relationship.

When we resolve to know one another and encourage one another without agendas and without fixing, the most natural response to an authentic sharing of life with a Godward orientation is to hit our knees *together*.

In fact, great spiritual friendships often develop a culture of prayer. In this kind of relationship, prayer is the immediate, obvious response. Friends know what kinds of circumstances will be difficult for each other, and they naturally move toward prayer. Soul friends pray for each other, even when they're apart.

But I wonder if the real fun doesn't begin until we pray together!

Friends pray together over e-mail, over the phone, in the back of train stations and in the front seats of minivans. They pray early and often. They pray in smoke-filled sports bars, they pray in flooded basements, they pray in expansive nature preserves, and they pray in crowded airports. They pray in times of confusion, temptation, aggravation and searing pain. They pray over new babies, new jobs, new opportunities and new houses. They pray, because prayer just makes sense as the way we respond to reality—to God—together.

During one particularly challenging season, one friend surmised that we had worn knee-holes in the carpet around my living room coffee table. I think she was right! And yet we both see how God moved powerfully in the weeks and months that followed. In times of bewildering circumstances, acute pain or debilitating patterns of self-destruction, we can talk and talk. But when we talk and pray, well, that engages a whole new level of spiritual power. Looking back, it's amazing to see what unfolded for each of us. I shudder to think, *Would things have gone differently if we hadn't prayed?* I don't need to know the answer; I'm just glad we did.

■ What role does prayer currently play in your friendships?

■ What would feel risky about suggesting a greater expression of prayer?

■ What could help you remember to pray together more frequently?

■ What do you think would change if you had a greater experience of prayer in friendship?

■ Use the remaining space to talk to God about this.

So we've looked at the vital roles of mirroring, of self-disclosure and confession, of giving and receiving grace, and of prayer. The last way to develop a soul friendship that we'll cover is celebration. In this context, I am not referring to the celebration of birthdays and such. This kind of celebration is actually a form of mirroring. Soul friends have the unique ability to celebrate the activity of God in each other's lives! We celebrate growth. We celebrate even the smallest glimpses of healing and life and God-given freedom.

During the lifelong process of growth and change, we tend to be blind to our own growth. In truth, we may be growing, softening, strengthening, but we don't see it. We only see how far we have to go or the huge barriers that still exist in our attempt to follow God.

We might become quickly discouraged and lose heart when we're facing the same ugly temptation we've been fighting for years. But friends can offer a different point of view: one that is life giving and hope filled, one that celebrates the activity of God and highlights even the smallest incremental movements of our soul—even in the midst of our struggle.

I know of one friend who struggled with debilitating resentment and routinely faced a long downward spiral when conflict arose in any close relationship. But her soul friend, upon hearing the most recent angry episode that left her disheartened and feeling hopeless, mirrored another truth alongside the fact of recurring anger. "It used to take six weeks or more before you'd get to this point of talking and praying about this conflict, and it's only been three days this time—that's progress! Do you see the activity of God and the way you're responding differently to him in the midst of this?"

Truthfully, we may not see what our friends see. That's why we need those loving mirrors.

Another important reason for celebration is this: God receives the glory and the praise for his intimate involvement in our lives! For his relentless pursuit of our hearts, for his power to overcome the darkness in our souls, for the truth we get to experience from Philippians 1:6: "being confident of this, that he who began a good work in you will carry it on to completion." He does, and he will, and our friends can help us see it, believe it, trust it and yield to it.

■ Think of one of your friends. Where have you seen him or her take courageous steps recently? Where have they stood firm against temptation? When have they expressed authentic brokenness or even confusion? Can you see the activity of God in those instances?

■ How can you affirm and celebrate both what God has done and the growth in your friend? Write out what you might say here.

■ Prayerfully reflect on one of your own areas of growth—what glimpses of God's activity might have gone unnoticed along the way? Stop right now to thank and praise him. Celebrate his goodness and energy and life.

4 SOUL SPELUNKING

As we discussed earlier, one of the finest examples of a soul friendship walks off the pages of Scripture in the story of two men (yes, these friendships need not be relegated to the "pink zone"). Their story is not presented as a how-to on soul friends, but we can certainly learn from their example.

Remember, David and Jonathan should not have been friends. They should have been adversaries, competitors seeking one another's demise. But that was not the case. God knit their hearts together. And despite being public figures, despite everything they could stand to lose because of their friendship, they ventured into a life-giving, intimate relationship that helped them pay attention to God.

How do we know?

One verse in particular represents a concise example of a healthy soul friendship in action. It's a small verse, but one that packs a big message for anyone who wants to delve more deeply into spiritual friendship: "Saul's son Jonathan went to David at Horesh and helped him find strength in God" (1 Samuel 23:16).

■ Take a little time to read the surrounding text. Why was David in Horesh?

■ What do you notice about their friendship from this verse?

What a striking example, and in many ways it relates to the friendships we can offer one another. How? Well, like David, we all feel pain over various circumstances in our lives or from our past experiences. It could be the pain of rejection or betrayal in marriage or ministry. It could, like with David, be the very real threat of an enemy. It could be fear over the future of a child. It could be the loss of a pregnancy. It could be depression. It could be any number of things, but we all encounter pain in this life.

What do we do when we're in pain? We run and hide. Sometimes we protect ourselves from a real threat as David did. Sometimes we just hide where we think no one will find us. And though we don't typically hide in caves anymore, we do still hide in many other ways. Maybe your cave is your career or the identity of your ministry. It may be shopping, exercise or eating. I've hidden behind my children; I've hidden behind my work. You may even hide in a friendship, staying at a comfortable surface level when what you really need is to go deeper.

Think about your own life for a minute, then answer these questions.

■ What are, or have been, primary sources of pain in your life?

■ Under what circumstances do you experience fear?

■ Where you tend to "hide"?

■ What does it generally take to "find you" there?

Somehow, Jonathan knew David was in trouble, knew where David would be when he felt threatened, and he went there without being summoned. Soul friends can do that. They know when you're hurting and afraid. They know how to break through your resistances. They know where to find you.

Once there, however, did you notice what Jonathan did? Or, more importantly, didn't do? Soul friends do a very unique thing: They help you find strength in God. They do not try to fix you. They do not try to convince you everything is okay. They do not try to be God for you. They are not even concerned primarily with helping you get happy again. They want to help reconnect you with God, which is what you most need in that moment. What did that look like for David? We have no idea!

Finding strength in God takes many forms, since each of us derives strength differently. It might look like a time of intimate conversation, shedding tears and praying together. At the other extreme, it might be silence. But believe it or not, it might involve a movie, a bowl of ice cream, steaming hot tea or an ice-cold beer. (Are you feeling more qualified yet?) It may look like a trip to the botanical gardens. It may look like offering to care for young children so a friend can take a nap or helping that person drywall the basement.

But make no mistake: a soul friend's ultimate goal is to help a person find strength in the only final source of strength that exists—God. Keep in mind, a friend in pain may not want anything to do with God, but just by being present, you're connecting with their soul. Flawed and broken as you are, you just brought an essential piece of God right to the heart of your friend—just by showing up. That indwelling dynamic is at work. The rest is up to God.

■ What helps you find strength in God?

- How well do any of your friends know about both your places of strength and pain?

- How well could you answer these same questions for your friend? Do you know when they're in pain or afraid? Do you know where their "cave" is? Do you know what it takes to find them there? Do you know what helps them find strength in God? Are you willing to simply show up with no agenda?

5 GROUP DISCUSSION

Summary

For many people, taking a next step in developing some soul friends involves prayer. Whether requesting that God would provide someone with whom to build a soul friendship, or together with a soul friend, seeking his presence and power for the realities of life, prayer just makes sense. When the Holy Spirit moves among us and through us, the growth trajectory of our souls takes a turn in the right direction! And as a friendship like this deepens, it makes sense to celebrate—to acknowledge the activity of God, to celebrate the growth and healing and transformation, however seemingly incremental and small. Miracles come in all sizes, and just a little less anger or a little more compassion signifies something special. God receives the recognition and acknowledgment that all this comes from him, is produced in human souls by him, and ultimately reflects his character and purposes on earth. Like Jonathan and David from ancient times, soul friends meet one another in the realities of life and help one another connect meaningfully with our truest source of strength—God. Because we embrace this way of relating, we end up doing the kinds of things God would do, for the reasons God would do them, in the way God would do them. We extend, by his power, his trinitarian community of oneness here on earth.

Opening

How have you been doing since we last gathered as a group?

Discussion

1. What, if anything, did you sense God stirring in you through this final experience?

2. Go back over your written responses to parts one through four. What one or two ideas stand out as something you'd like to bring to the group? Why did they stand out to you?

3. Return to "Part Two: Praying with a Spiritual Friend." Describe your responses to the questions in that section.

4. How has your experience in this group helped you understand the dynamics of spiritual friendships?

5. If you feel comfortable, describe some of your responses to the questions about what kinds of pain cause you to hide in "caves," that is, what are your sources of pain, and what tends to be your cave?

6. What is one step you can take in the next thirty days to forge or deepen a spiritual friendship?

Prayer

Since this is your last group time, be sure to take a few minutes to discuss each person's desire, if any, for further study or interaction. Maybe a new discussion guide would be best. Or perhaps it would be fun to go to a movie or share a relaxed meal or evening together. Whatever it is, be sure to celebrate your learning together and thank one another for the gift of your growing connections.

Have one or several group members close this time in prayer.

CONCLUSION

In a relationship with God, we have a friend in Jesus—a never-changing, never-wrong, never-inappropriate, never-sinful friend. And yet God has designed the spiritual life in such a way that he intends to show up in your life through the eyes and the ears and the voice and the tears of flesh-and-blood people—a few intentionally pursued soul friends.

Unlike God, we will change. We are sometimes wrong. We may occasionally be inappropriate, and we certainly will sin. But spiritual friendships are a significant way to care for our souls and ultimately to experience the kind of life God has made available to us: a life of purpose, deep joy and contentment, increasing strength, goodness, and yieldedness to God.

Hopefully, as you've gone through this book, you have discovered or deepened connections to a few soul-companions. Together, you will grow and stretch and "run hard after God."

Where will you go from here? Several additional core spiritual practices will be important for the spiritual journey that lies ahead—time-honored ways to care for your soul. For example, you might want to look for resources on new ways of prayer, experiment with creative journaling, delve into solitude, silence or even self-examination. Or you may need to get more time outdoors, find a church community or discover a place to serve others. As you explore these and other ways to care for your soul, you may also want to check out the other Soul Care Resources guide, *Discovering Soul Care,* and visit <www.soul care.com>.

Rather than giving you a list of religious "to-dos," it is my prayer that you will find great joy and deep peace as you find authentic ways to connect your soul to God, our source of life.